Stronger than Metal

The Love of Chris and Lewis

LEWIS T. BERSHELL

Fulton Books, Inc.
Meadville, PA

Published by Fulton Books 2020

ISBN 978-1-64952-111-8 (paperback)
ISBN 978-1-64952-112-5 (digital)

Printed in the United States of America

Chapter One

We believe that we are, to coin the phrase "two different sides of the same coin." According to this definition, from google, "If *two* things are *two sides of the same coin* or *opposite sides of the same coin*, they are closely related to each other and cannot be separated, even though they seem to be completely different." What we need to determine is do we meet this definition?

Christine Kaye Mohr is the name given to her by her parents—father Andrew Jackson Mohr Junior and mother Margaret Lucille Applegate. Her father's family came to America from Germany and settled the northern part of Shelby County in Indiana. They owned and farmed all that land. Margaret Lucille Applegate was the granddaughter of Lucretia Brooks, who was the owner of southern Hamilton County in Indiana. Christine came from what is known in America as the white race. She was raised with the belief that she was entitled to whatever she wanted. She came from wealth on both sides of her family; according to *Ancestry*, her mother's family can be traced back to the king of Scotland.

Lewis Terrell Bershell is the name given to me by my parents, father Sammie Bershell Junior and mother Christella Watson; my family as with most families is what was known in America as African American, or black people. My mother's side of the family can be traced back to Dublin, Ireland. My fathers' side of the family has no connection pass Georgia. I was raised by my great-grandparents, Jimmie Hall and Nettie Clay. When you looked at Jimmie Hall, he looked like any other white man in the south. He was the oldest son in a mulatto family. He seems to have been added to the family. He often told me that his own father, Alex Hall, could not whip him:

when he got into trouble, he would run to the Campbell place. I do remember that papa had a connection with the most powerful lawyers in the city of Bastrop, Louisiana.

Papa and mama cosigned for a car for my father. He skipped town with and stopped making the payments. The car dealer came after mama and papa for the payment and started getting nasty, because he thought he was dealing with black people. In the Jim Crow south, he could say or do whatever he wants to, from a legal perspective. Jimmie Hall was not your normal member of the black race of people in Bastrop, Louisiana. He was connected to some of the most powerful families in Bastrop, Louisiana. His legal connection was the lawyers, from the Madison family. After one trip to his lawyers, the car dealer made no more contact with mama and papa. Papa's two sons, William Terrell Hall and Morris Jimmie Hall, left Bastrop and became very successful.

When I was twelve years old, Mama and I spent the summer with uncle Jimmie and aunt Lula in Hayward, California. The summer spent with uncle Jimmie changed my whole life. Uncle Jim started changing the way I responded to people the day he met us at the train station. During the summer in Hayward, I played with a mixture of kids; my best friend was biracial white Japanese Patrick—a little white boy who wanted very much to be my friend, but I was not accustomed to being friends with white kids. I have always remembered Danny and Pam. Danny was a year older than me, and his sister Pam was a year younger than me. Their parents as like most of the white families living around us who had a very good relationship with Papa.

Their parents, Mr. and Mrs. Harrington, had their wooden home tore down and replace with a brick house; the lumber from the old house was given to Papa, which was used to build an addition on our house. Their children, Danny and Pam, became friends with me. They moved away, and I have never forgotten the friendship and longed for another friendship with white kids.

I was often teased and threatened by the black boys I went to school with. I believed in avoiding fighting, for two reasons: (1) Fighting always caused you to get a whipping from the principle.

In the black school, every teacher used either a strap, which was a portion of a fan belt from a car, or a board with holes drilled into it. There was nothing that anyone could do that would cause me to experience that treatment. (2) I believed in the teaching of Jesus, since I was raised in the church, and became one of the first junior deacons, at The Greater Magnolia Baptist Church. The black girls avoided me because of how the boys treated me. They often teased each other about liking me. And the response was, "I do not like, Bershell." There has always been a degree of racism in black people. I am having very light skinned or described as high yellow and was only interested in girls with skin color as my own. Part of the problem was that in another world and another time, Pam and I could have had a relationship. That was a world twenty years away.

When our school system was integrated, I was a member of the first integrated class that graduated from Bastrop High School, the original white school. The old black school, which was first named Morehouse Training School and had all twelve grades on the same campus, was turned into a junior high school. Bastrop High School was the first time I felt at home in school, and I also noticed that I had caught the eyes of some of the white girls. My light skin color, being so close to white, was not as much of a change as dark skin color. Therefore, members of my family had turned white and made sure there was no connection to black people, because of the danger to them if discovered.

This reminded me of the 1951 movie *Showboat*. Where Ava Gardner, who played the part of a woman, the star female performer, had to leave the show because she had a trace of black bloodlines, and it was against the law, in the southern states along the Mississippi River, where the boat traveled. The ability to blend into the white race was only done by women, which was easier because of the relationship that white men and black women had with each other. Black men and white women were always kept apart and discourage by the death of the black man.

One day, we had band practice outside. I was sitting beside a white girl whose name was Janet; when there was a bee that landed above her knee, she was terrified, and as a reaction, I just knocked it off her. She was very grateful to me for saving her, from getting stung by that bee. In knocking the bee off her, I had touched her also. Janet was two grades behind me; there was an interest between us, but it was still way too soon. A relationship at that time would have caused me to be visited by the local and KKK and then hung. From then on, in my life, my interest was in white women, until I finally found Chris. My marriage to Mattie was an act of desperation because of low self-esteem, and my need for a mother, after Mama died.

When I graduated, in order to achieve the success that I wanted in life, I had to leave Louisiana. My parents lived in Rockford, Illinois, and came down to my graduation, and I returned to Rockford with them. I graduated at the age of seventeen and would not turn eighteen until December; the great jobs in factories were not available to me, because I had to be eighteen to work in a factory. When I turned eighteen, the job market had dried up.

I had to return to Bastrop to register for the draft and received an A1 rating and would have been drafted in Louisiana, which was not good for me. I went to the Army recruiter in Rockford and learned that if I enlisted, I could be guaranteed the job I wanted in the Army. I decided to go to Chicago to be tested but didn't past the entrance exam. My recruiter sent me to classes for a week in Chicago, to prepare for the next test. Upon completion of the next test, I was able to get scores high enough to become a clerk typist in the US Army.

I packed my bag, said goodbye to my family, and went to the Armed Forces Induction Center in Chicago to take my physical exam and then enlist in the US Army on April 14, 1971. That night, we boarded charter buses and went to the O'Hare International Airport. We waited in a special area of the airport and then boarded a charter airplane, bound for Seattle, Washington. We then boarded charter buses to Fort Lewis, where I completed my basic military training.

While in training, I hurt my ankle, and I was put on a three-day restriction and couldn't run in the morning. I made the restriction last a week, but when I had to run again, I fell behind along with others; we paid the price later when we were forced to run back to the company area with full gear. After eight weeks, I graduated and shipped out bound for Fort Ord, California. I spent eight weeks there in clerk school, where I became a clerk typist.

After graduating, I received orders assigning me to the finance school at Fort Benjamin Harrison, Indiana. When I graduated from the finance school after eight weeks, I would have normally gone to Vietnam, but my class was mostly national guard and Army reserve students, and they were going back home. I received orders assigning me to the fourth finance company, fourth Infantry Division at Fort Carson, Colorado.

When I got there, they assigned me to a pay team, which maintains the financial records of service members stationed at the Fourth Infantry Division, at Fort Carson. My job title was pay dispersing specialist. The senior specialist that I worked with soon received his discharge from the Army and then left me with a mess that overwhelmed me.

The entire Army pay system went through a total change. My first assignment was to the files, which all I did was pull the records and file them back in their alphabetical location; I hated this job, and it showed in my work performance. I was then moved to the customer service branch where I became a specialist in allotment inquiries. An allotment is a set amount of money deducted from a service member's pay and sent to a designated payee.

My job was to call the finance and accounting center in Indianapolis and get a report on the activity of the allotment. I would use the government communication system, called Autovon. The system was very busy most of the time, because the finance center received calls from all over the world. I became very good at it and develop a relationship with a military pay clerk by the name of Mattie Ruth Busby. She later became my first wife.

Chapter Two

I worked on the midnight shift, at the Army Finance and Accounting Center, on Fort Benjamin Harrison, Indiana. I heard of the new data processing clerk, Christine K. Harris. She was creating a fuss about her shift assignment to the evening shift. She was under the impression that she was to work the day shift. Unwillingly, she went to the evening shift where our paths crossed during a change of shifts where we exchanged information.

During these exchanges, I notice that there was something about her that made me nervous. This was because I was married and so was she and after spending twenty-seven months in Germany and another eighteen months at Fort Knox, Kentucky, away from my wife while in the US Army. After seven years, two months, and twenty-seven days, I received my discharge from the Army and was hired under the veteran's readjustment act at the US Army Finance and Accounting Center, where Mattie worked, where she spent hours talking to me on the telephone, when I was stationed at Fort Carson, Colorado. I knew how to be a faithful husband to my wife. I also was the Youth Minister and creator of the Junior Church at the Kingsley Terrace Church of Christ.

When I met Chris, Mattie and I had been married for six years and had made it through the forced separation because of my military assignment. I held Mattie totally responsible for our separation. When we were married, she was forty-five years old, and I was twenty-two. She had three sons: the oldest, Lester, was two years older than me, and Michael was six months older than me, but I was six months older than Steven, her youngest. During our marriage. Mattie's commitment was to her mother, Minnie Clyde Clifford, and her sons, not our marriage. I never felt like a husband. But because of my military background, my actions demanded the respect of one and created a lot of problems for her.

Nowadays, an older woman is referred to as a cougar; in the case with Mattie and me, I was the one who tore down all her resistance. I reenlisted in the Army to get reassigned to Fort Knox, Kentucky, to get closer to her and drove across the country to be closer to her and then would drive four hours on weekends to see her. I bought the rings and set up the marriage arrangement. Then, the crushing thing happened: I got orders sending me to Germany.

On Thanksgiving Day of 1974, I landed in Frankfurt, Germany. Now, as a newlywed, I was having Thanksgiving dinner away from my new wife and family. This was worse than spending Christmas eve walking around a building on guard duty, on Fort Carson, Colorado. On guard duty, during the evening hours, I made friends with the bunny rabbits that ran about the place, but after midnight, I was all alone, they had gone to bed, and I felt abandoned even by the bunnies. Mattie Ruth Busby and I were married because I was a lonely soldier and had been away from any family for the last three years and would spend the next two years and three months the extra time that was added to the two-year unaccompanied tour.

This was more painful for me than being alone. It was my pursuit of Mattie that led to me being stationed in Germany. My assignment to the Fourth Infantry Division, Fourth Finance section, Fort Carson, Colorado, kept me from going to Vietnam. I would have spent the remainder of my enlistment at Fort Carson. The mission of the Fourth Infantry Division was to deploy to Germany in twenty-four hours, if war broke out between the East and West. The only way to leave Fort Carson was to reenlist for a new assignment or to be discharged from the Army. I reenlisted to get closer to Mattie.

My reassignment to Fort Knox, Kentucky, opened me up for this overseas assignment. Vietnam was no longer a possibility, because our troops were being withdrawn. I push the marriage because I didn't want to go to Germany before we were married and hoped she would travel with me. But this was not going to happen: she would not leave her mother and youngest son Steven to be with me. I traveled to Frankfurt, Germany, with families that would spend the next three years touring Europe.

She would never join me in Germany, and we had many heated words about why she would not come. I began preaching to cope with the loneliness from the separation. I had many opportunities to be unfaithful to her, but I never did. I even counsel an older seargent, my father's age, on the same subject. The man had cheated on his wife for his entire marriage; he even cheated with his neighbor's wife. He told me how he had to justify the money used to cover an abortion of one woman he had gotten pregnant. I did learn something from him that I would use later. The man said, "I can get any woman I want; there will always be a moment of weakness to use." I never forgot those words.

Chris and I worked together for the next five years and became very much aware of the relationship that was developing between us. She had pictures of her and her husband Jim on her desk, and I also had pictures of Mattie and me on mine. My coworker on her shift was Katheryn, an older woman who would make mistakes that I would correct. We had a very good working relationship, since Katheryn made the runs into the computer room, which gave me the time to work on my schoolwork.

Under the Veteran's Readjustment Assistance Act, I needed to earn college credits, which enabled me to be hired without taking the civil service exam. So, I was working on a degree in computer programming. I attended classes from 18:00 to 22:00 military time. The midnight or first shift was perfect for my schedule; getting enough sleep is the only problem. The reason is that the day shift was used by the programmers for testing and customer service, of all the operations in the building.

The two-night shifts were used for production. The jobs were started during the evening shift and were completed on the midnight to 8 a.m. shift. Data processing clerks provided an itemized listing of each item produced by the computer and its representatives, from areas of the building, would come and sign the itemized listing, and returned to their areas. When the paychecks and statement for the Army were under production, there was no idle time, and overtime was required to be worked. The rest of the month had a lot of free time. This is when I did my schoolwork.

Chris was assigned to the midnight shift of a period, switching with Katheryn, and the relationship between us grew even more. We even began to have rubber band wars, where we would shoot each other with rubber bands. We had a great working relationship. One of our favored tasks that could only be done at night when the building was empty was repossessing the carts that other sections had not returned. We would go all over the huge building; this is the Army's biggest building, next to the Pentagon. We also talked about our marriages and problems.

Chris as well as everyone else that I worked with knew that I was a minister. My dress was suits and ties; on an occasion, she decided to seek my counsel as a minister about her marital problems. I remembered the words of the older sergeant in Germany, "There is always a weak moment, in a woman." Now, here it is: I am now ready to pursue a serious relationship with her. She was also ready to pursue a relationship with me; this is the reason she let me know there was trouble in her marriage. We had spent many hours talking about our marriages. I told her how I felt that Mattie had destroyed our marriage.

She, on the other hand, knew that she would have never let me spend four years of marriage to her, away from me. She would have loved to live in Germany and taken advantage of the opportunity to tour Europe with me and the family we would create. She had lived her whole life in the Indianapolis area and envied me for all the places that I had lived in. She knew that if she had been my wife, I would have completed my military career. She knew that I only got out because of Mattie's refusal to travel with me. She knew that I was tired of being faithful to Mattie and looking for a replacement, and so was she.

The sad day came when she had to go back to the day shift. I would often hide in the corridor that ran beside the computer room and the outside windows to the inner court, to ambush her when she came to work in the mornings. Katheryn, because of health and age, was forced to retire again; she had retired earlier and had to return to work for the government after her husband passed away. Chris then received a permanent assignment to the midnight shift. Everyone on the midnight shift was happy for us and felt that we deserved each other. Even people on the day shift knew about us. We soon picked up where we had left off in our relationship.

In the break area were jigsaw puzzles that everyone worked on. We really got into working the puzzles together. We even started looking for more challenging puzzles and decided to go on a road trip after work, to Louisville, Kentucky. By now, our relationship has really grown. We were working on a puzzle that was so hard that no one else wanted to mess with it. So, we worked it together, and when it got close to being finish, I planned to share the first kiss with her, to celebrate the completion of the puzzle. She knew it was coming and was ready.

Now, it became clear: our relationship is physical and could be considered a love affair, which caused us to have a conversation about where we wanted it to go. We both knew that we both had finally found the one we were looking for, at ages thirty-three and thirty-two, with no children by anyone else. We didn't want to be away from each other anymore. She told me that she did not want to go back to Jim. I had never felt so helpless in my life. What could I do?

We had nowhere to stay and no money. Our coworkers and friends were very much aware of our situation. They were concerned for the safety of Chris, because Jim had a pass of hitting her. Jean came up with a solution. She offered us the use of the second bedroom in her home.

We both went home and loaded our cars with our clothing and moved to Jean's house, on the northwest side of Indianapolis, on Michigan Road. We were far away from everyone, which became our safe haven. We moved on Thursday morning and did not have to go to work on Friday night, which would be Saturday morning. Saturday was hard on us: we started feeling guilty for what we had done. We had blindsided the two people whom we had spent many years with, nine for her and eleven for me.

Sunday morning, she needed to leave for a while, and when she returned, she informed me that she was going back to Jim. By noon, she was gone, and I was alone. I had a flashback of my junior year of high school. My girlfriend Lilly, her best friend, and I were sitting together in the auditorium at an all-day drama competition. Shella and her girlfriend were coming down the row and sat right on the side of me. My girlfriend became aware of my interest in Shella. After the lunch break, I was alone and had neither. This is the situation that I am now in with Mattie.

Chris had decided to leave Jim for me, but now, she was not sure this was best for her. She found herself in a world where she was totally out of place. All her life she grew up in and lived in the white world. She had little contact with black people. This world that she is now part of had always been referred to as they and them. She knew how her family would react to this and would never accept me—not just her parents and sister, but her whole family.

She remembered that the Mohr's, her father's side of the family, had come to this country from Germany and settled northern Shelby County and owned all that land. Her mother came from the Brooks family, who goes back to The King of Scotland. She was also concerned that if she got pregnant, would Lewis be as what she heard about black men getting white girls pregnant with biracial children to be raised alone? She knew if I left her, her family would never accept the baby, and she would be alone with nowhere to go.

Jim was wanting to talk to her, so she decided to go meet with him. When she met with him, he gave her no reason to fear him. He had hit her before and really beat up his first wife, the mother of his children. Jim wanted her to come home. And if she did, he would let her do what she always wanted: to quit work. He was giving her a chance to return to her world and end this nightmare that she had gotten herself into. So, she went and told me and then left me alone.

I could not believe what had just happened. She was really gone, and now, I had been rejected again, and what all women had done in my life was causing me pain, except for one: Mattie, who had always been there for me. When Mama died, in January 1974, I needed no one else but Mattie. I had traveled from Fort Knox, Kentucky, on a bus, got stuck at the bus station, in Pine Bluff, Arkansas, for a day, because of an ice storm that shut down the roads in southern Arkansas and Northern Louisiana.

After the funeral, I traveled all the way to Indianapolis, just to spend the evening with Mattie, before going back south to Fort Knox, Kentucky. I have no other family member in this state, let alone Indianapolis; my only family was Mattie.

I knew that I couldn't stay with Jean, so I called Mattie, and she agreed to talk with me. So, I drove over, and she came out and got in the car with me. I told her I was sorry for the way I had treated her and that I had done a stupid thing. I asked her if she would take me back. Just like Jim, Mattie let me come home.

I did not have to go to work that night, because I was on leave. I had heard that Chris's last day at work was Friday, so I would never see her again. The next day, Monday, I was very busy, because the sewer had backed up again, because of the roots. I rented a drain cleaner and cleaned the drain.

Living in this old house, I had learned to do many things. I had learned how to run electrical wire from the electrician that I hired to rewire the house. The electrical wiring in this old house was dangerous. The need for an electrician came, when the back porch and the detached garage, with its burned-out roof, were condemned by the board of health. I without getting permission from the owner, Mattie's mother, hired a crew to tear down the garage and removed the back porch. With the back porch gone, the electrical box was outside and exposed to the weather, which made the electrical problem worse.

I hired an old electrician by the name of Parkee. Parkee also taught me all about running electrical wiring. When Parkee finished the job, I knew how to wire for an electric dryer, of which I did later. Mattie's mother (Clyde Clifford) protested, but it had no effect on any of the decisions I made around there.

I felt that I had spent four years of my marriage, because Mattie would not leave this woman, and now, for the same reason, I was forced to live in this old house that they had let get in this shape. And her son Steven, with the same age as me, did nothing around there. Later, I replace the kitchen sink and added a dishwasher and washer. I ran hot- and cold-water lines and sewer lines in the kitchen. The toilet needed replacing, of which the floor and connection to the toilet bowl had to be replaced. I installed wall-to-wall carpet in the entire house.

The thing that really upset Mattie's mother was when I decided to create a parking place and driveway in the back. I bought a dump truck load of gravel, had it dumped in the back yard, and hired some guys in the neighborhood to spread the gravel for the parking place and driveway. I have never forgotten the expression on her face when the dump truck lifted its bed and unloaded the gravel in piles because it couldn't spread it because of the power lines running to the house. I didn't care what that old woman thought, because I had spent some of the loneliest days of my life because of her.

My tour of Germany was worse than the Christmas eve that I spent walking around on guard duty at Fort Carson, Colorado 2000 miles away from home. As I walked around that building, an old museum, there were bunny rabbits all around the area; they became my friend. I looked forward to seeing them as I made my rounds. Then, on the shift for two to four o'clock in the morning, they had gone to bed, and now, I really felt alone. To a soldier away from home and family, a mail call is one of the most important things to him. And Mattie was lazy about writing so I went to many mail calls and got nothing.

When Mattie got home from work, I was nowhere to be found: I would not be at school. Because I did not have class on Thursday night, plus I was always home when she got home. I went to class after she got home. When she got to our bedroom and found my clothing gone, she knew I had gone. Currently, Mattie had never really been alone, and now, she was. Her being alone was worse than mine, because in the Army, the term "band of brothers" means that you become connected to people whom you would never have a connection—you become a family where you are never alone; when I received my discharge from the Army, even going home to my family, I really felt more alone than when I was in Germany.

She was aware of the relationship that I had with Chris. The husband of a lady she had worked with for years was the computer room supervisor on the shift that I and Chris worked. Our growing relationship was known, by many. The Finance Center had thousands of government employees, but Mattie was part of a close group of employees, who had known about me for years. They had encouraged her in the relationship and marriage to me.

When she met me for the first time, she traveled from Indianapolis to Rockford, Illinois, with her three sons. I was home on leave and would be going back the same day. She was terrified that I would reject her; she didn't look in person as young as she did in the pictures I had of her, which did disappoint me. But I didn't care; from talking to her on the phone every day, I had developed a relationship with her. They drove me to the airport in Chicago, where I flew back to Colorado.

Back at Fort Carson, I reenlisted on July 24, 1973, with a new duty station of Fort Knox, Kentucky. With the bonus I received, I bought a new car and drove across the country, alone to get closer to her. On the day I was leaving for Fort Knox, Kentucky, I drove Mattie to work and had an accident and had to spend an extra week in Indianapolis awaiting car repairs. While waiting, I stayed in an extra room at Mattie's house.

During the year, September 1973 to September 1974 that followed, I made the three-hour drive from Fort Knox, Kentucky, to Indianapolis twice a month and stayed in a local motel. When Mattie's middle son Michael graduated from the School of Arts and Design in Columbus, Ohio, I went with Mattie. A young woman asked Michael, "Just who is Lewis? He is with your mother." Michael reply was, "He is my mother's boyfriend." I kept trying to get Mattie to marry me, but she was not ready. On the first anniversary of my reenlistment, I received my annual bonus and decided to buy Mattie an engagement ring. I had received my orders to report to Germany on November 27, 1974. Mattie and I got married on August 14, 1974.

From November 27, 1974, to February 24, 1976, I was stationed in Aschaffenburg, Germany. I came home two times and called home every month. I felt that she should join me in Germany. But she was determined not to leave her mother and son, Steven.

When my tour of duty in Germany was complete, I returned to Fort Knox, Kentucky. I was there from March 24, 1976, to July 28. While stationed at Fort Knox, Kentucky, I came home every weekend. When I got out of the Army, I went to work at the Finance and Accounting Center with Mattie.

I was working in the basement when the mail came that evening. Mattie noticed that there was a letter addressed to me, from Chris. Mattie placed the letter on the table so that I could see it. Then, she waited for me to come up and see what I would do.

I came up and saw the letter, took it, went to the bedroom, and began to read it. By the time I finished, Mattie had come upstairs. She asked me about the letter, and I gave it to her to read. Her words were, "she is not going to let you go." The words haunted me, to the point that I would never let her go either. So, I decided to go back to work that night. I had made up my mind: that I would get her back whatever it took; I will spend the rest of my life with her.

When Chris got back home to Jim, she knew she had made a mistake in leaving me. She was reminded of it when she got to work, and he was not there. She had to tell everyone why she decided to leave him and go back to Jim. Lewis had a support group of older black women, and now, she had been accepted into the group. During the night, she wrote the letter to me and put it in the mail. To this day, we often wonder how she was able to mail a letter at Fort Harrison, and I got it in Indianapolis the same day. We have and do believe that there are forces involved in our lives that transcend human understanding.

As soon as we saw each other, we knew that we would never leave each other again. We started planning the next time we would leave Mattie and Jim. We both felt that we had given them both a chance, and now, we all knew that it was over. We made it through Thanksgiving with them, then loaded the cars again, and moved out. I went back and had a talk with Mattie. She decided that she would take care of the divorce.

We moved back into Jean's house again and made the most of the time. This was a new experience for Chris. When I got home from school one night, Chris met me in the hall with my pistol in her hand; all the activity that had been going on in the house had terrified her. From that night on, she went to school with me and stayed in the break area while I was in class.

This was a new experience for both of us; we were like two kids on their own for the very first time. We had no furniture, other than an old sofa sleeper that Jean had given us when we moved out of her house. There was a little drafting table that I had brought with me, which became our dining table; we picked up a couple of cheap folding chairs.

We got our first turkey, and neither one of us had any experience at cooking turkeys. Mattie and her mother had always cooked the turkeys, using the same method that I grew up with. Most of the time, it was a hen; turkeys were too big for this method: cooked in a pot of water, then put in a roasting pan, stuffed and surrounded with dressing then baked. This method left the bird dry and without flavor. I have never forgotten the flavor of the Thanksgiving dinners, especially the dressing that was served back in the school cafeteria. I spent the rest of my life trying to recreate the dressing from school.

Some of the Army mess halls came close. Thanksgiving was one of the times when the mess sergeants demonstrate their years of cooking skills; these were the best mess halls on the army base and would have long lines of those waiting to eat. But it was bread stuffing, which to me was gummy. This was the method taught in the Army cook school that was at Fort Ord, California, in 1971. Jim was a navel cook and always cooked the turkeys in Chris's home. We decided that we needed to learn how to do our own holiday cooking. This is the beginning of our *Bershell Family Recipe Book.* We created our own method of preparing our favored foods, based upon our research.

When Chris's family found out about me, they did just as we expected: no way was I going to be allowed into their house. Her sister Carolyn was the worst and had the nastiest thing to say about me. Chris made it clear to them: they would accept me, or they would lose her forever, and she meant it too. This commitment was what I had dreamed of in a wife: she knew that it would always end up with just the two of us, counting on each other. She would for the rest of our lives have my back, and I would have hers (I'm not saying these things about the future; this is what has happened over the last thirty years).

On February 24, 1986, Chris and Jim went before the judge to finalize their divorce. He had his youngest son with him, Chris was alone, but I was waiting across the street at the farmer's market. My divorce was delayed because Mattie's attorney was slow in setting up the court date. He was a member of the church where I was the youth minister, and they wanted me to return to her. The belief of the Church was that they would be forced to "withdraw from me, according to their interpretation of the new testament." I made a visit to the attorney's office, and since I was paying half of his fee, I expected him to get the divorce completed.

On Monday, March 9, 1986, Mattie and I went before the judge to finalize our divorce. She had her sister and youngest son with her, and I was alone, but Chris was waiting across the street at the farmer's market, just as I had for her. On Friday, March 14, 1986, we were married in Rockford, Illinois, with my family around us. We went to Rockford because in Indiana there was a waiting period, and we had waited long enough. Plus, Nettie Lucretia Bershell would arrive on March 7, 1987.

Chapter Three

The two marriages had accumulated a lot of debt; I had agreed to pay everything except the car payment of which Mattie was driving. Chris took on her car payment and a loan that her motorcycle was attached to. She loved that little Honda of hers. I can remember the coldest day in December with a temperature of thirty degrees Fahrenheit, and she rode it across town to bring it home. When she got home, she was frozen. That summer, we had so much fun riding it. She was the driver, and I rode on the back. We spent the entire day on it.

The next day, I was ready to go again, but she said that she couldn't go out in the sun anymore. That's when I really learned about sunburns. The term "lobster" was first used. While in the Army, I had many white friends, and I knew about sunburns. Even with my very light skin color and growing up in Louisiana, I had never had one and was not affected by anyone who had one. Black people have an ingredient in our skin that protects us from the effect of the sun, but we always stay in the shade, and people who lived in the south covered exposed areas of their bodies. At the pool in the apartment complex where we lived, there were many sunbathers.

That year, the Indy 500 race was rained out and had to be rescheduled to the next weekend; this caused a lot of race fans to hang around the area for a week. At the Lafayette Square mall, we saw a lot of bad sunburns. But with Chris, I felt that I had caused her this discomfort. I realized that her skin was really damaged; she had trouble sleeping. Luckily, it was just her face, arms, and legs. She told me, while they were in Hawaii, she got a sunburn so bad that her hair got caught in a blister; she really had sun poisoning.

From then on, when we went to the pool, we would always sit in the shade of an umbrella. I have been very protective of her. Speaking of sunburns, our oldest grandson Gabriel has blond hair and blue eyes and looks very white, but he does not burn. In fact, both he and his younger brother Michael can stay in the swimming pool all day, without sunshield, and not burn.

We found that our incomes were not enough to cover our bills, even using a bill management company. They were only concerned about the credit cards, which would be wiped out from bankruptcy, and not the secured loans. We decided that the only way was to file for bankruptcy and get a new start. We had to let the cars and motorcycle go. This was hurtful to Chris. The first time I met James Harris, her ex-husband, was when she turned over the car and motorcycle to him. After that meeting, she never saw him again. With the burden of all that debt gone, we were able to get a car from a buy-here, pay-here car lot. That old Ford LTD turned out to be a good buy. We made several trips to Rockford and three trips to Bastrop Louisiana.

When we got the positive pregnancy test, Madea, Daddy, my brother Donald, and sister-in-law Linda were all excited. Chris's family was very upset. Her mother and sister wanted her to get an abortion. That hurt her so much: the child she had wanted so bad was so rejected. Her father had an accident with the lawnmower; we went over to check on him, and he met me for the first time.

He decided to take us to a little café down the street; there were only the white people whom he knew in there, he had exposed his son-in-law to his world, and that broke the ice between us. From that day forward, we became father and son: I grew closer to him than I was to my own dad; he became the replacement of Papa to me. I never called him anything but Dad. We spent the rest of the day together at his house.

When her mother and sister got home, Carolyn came in and went right back out. When I first saw her, I thought she was Chris; they look so much alike. I met Mom for the first time and have never called her anything else but Mom. Carolyn was next, who didn't take much after Mom. All the members of her family began to fall like dominoes: Aunt Deloris, Mom's sister, and her husband Uncle

Lawrence. Uncle Lawrence stated his feelings about interracial marriage, and that was it. He was a gun enthusiast; he even took me to the gun club of which he was a member.

Now, Chris had the support during her pregnancy that she needed. Every Sunday, we all met for Sunday dinner, either at their house or at a restaurant, of which they always picked up the tab. That summer at the state fair, I met Whity the doctor, who was a Shriner clown, Chris's uncle Sam. Chris's family were exhibitors, at the Indiana state fair. Mom was an expert at making pies; once you tasted one of her pies, you wouldn't find another to equal it. Carolyn received the Land O'lakes award at the state fair. Dad created a new category in growing the tallest sunflower: eighteen feet.

The first time we went to Bastrop to see papa, we were very nervous, traveling through the small towns in Mississippi and Louisiana. I took my new wife around to everyone who knew me. We visited a cousin, Omega Brooks, whose house I spent a lot of time at while growing up; she was the mother of a cousin my Daddy had grown up with. She often told me about older women getting involved with younger men, and what did I do? Marry Mattie and bring her right to her house.

When I showed up with Chris, she called to her son-in-law Eddie and said, "Hey Eddie, Lewis got rid of that old woman." And Eddie's reply was, "Yeah, and got a white one now." Eddie and his son Leo were almost like business partners in WC Deboss and Son Janitorial Service.

After graduating from high school on one of my trips back to Bastrop, I worked for them for a while. We cleaned the offices around the town, on an occasion while washing windows; some white girls whom I had gone to school with drove by and yelled in a playful manner, "Work, my slaves. Work." And one of the guys I was working with said, "Yeah, baby. We are your slaves." We all got a great laugh behind this, because no one was offended, from the entire exchange. From that point on, I made up my mind—that I would work behind a desk for the rest of my working life.

Whenever I was in town, Ellis Whitmore always found me; this time he brought his wife Linda, so the four of us made plans to go to the city of Monroe, which had not happened before while I was married to Mattie. Linda was a year older than Ellis and me, and Chris is thirteen months younger than me, so we are all in the same age group, not like Mattie, which would be like having our mother along on a date; she was older than my mother and his mother too.

But the trip never happened because Chris got sick, and I had to take her to the local hospital. I was out in the yard talking to my friend, Buddy, when papa came and got me. Chris has often talked about how concerned papa was about and kept checking on her. She was getting dehydrated, and this was not caused by morning sickness from her pregnancy, but from a viral infection; she needed intravenous therapy.

At the hospital, there I was sitting beside her bed (a white girl, pregnant by a black man, in a hospital in Bastrop, Louisiana, a place only a decade ago, which would have cost me my life). Things started changing in Bastrop, after my graduating class in 1970; as early as 1972, there were relationships between white girls and black boys. These relationships were done in secret because the white parents had not changed. From my government health insurance, we could afford for her to be treated in this hospital.

Chris ended up quitting her job because the physical demands caused problems with her pregnancy. We also had moved to an apartment closer to where the family was. Dad and I were working on the old barn when Chris went into labor. On March 7, 1987, Nettie Lucretia Bershell was born. We named her after our two great-grandmothers: Nettie Hall and Lucretia Applegate. I will never forget the look in Mom's eyes, as she held her granddaughter for the first time. Nettie was always treated like a third daughter to her.

When we left the hospital with our new little baby daughter, I became so overwhelmed with the thought of our new responsibility that my nervous stomach caused me to pull the car over, where I threw up, but we were not alone for Mom, Dad, and Carolyn were waiting for us when we got home. They were always there to help us, with whatever we needed for as long as they lived.

With the loss of Chris's income, Dad got me a part-time job at the Washington Square shopping mall. He was the maintenance supervisor at J.C. Penney's. They needed the break room painted, so he hired me to do the job. I was very nervous, because they knew that I was his son-in-law and would not let him help me with the job. He would come in during his breaks and tell me what I needed to do. Dad and I also worked together on projects, such as building carports.

Chris and I decided to make another trip to see Papa and let him see Nettie our daughter named after his wife; we made the trip back to the south again. We decided this time to use a local motel, because of the heat, and it would be easier for our new baby to be in an air-conditioned environment. My father and my brother and his son, my nephew, were also down there. We were able to get a picture of the four generations, one with papa holding the child my family thought that I would never have.

Chapter Four

One of the things that Chris, Mom, and Carolyn wanted to do was to enter Nettie in baby pageants. While still a toddler, Nettie was entered in baby pageants. Mom and Dad took care of the entry fees and the little dresses she wore. Chris is expecting our son Andrew Terrell Bershell now; during the time of her pregnancy, certain events took place in our lives: Papa passed away, and we went to Bastrop for the last time.

My father-in-law's brother, Uncle Russell, passed away, and I met for the first time many members of the family, who had been waiting to meet me. I had been the talk of the Mohr family: Christine's first husband was an old man according to her mother and was going to have him arrested on their wedding day; she had led the police to believe that her daughter was underage, but Chris was over twenty-one and could marry whomever she wishes. Now, she has married and had a baby by a member of the black race.

But when they met me and our daughter, everything they were led to believe was wrong. Nettie, who was thirteen months old, and her eight-year-old second cousin hung out together during the funeral at the funeral home.

Our son Andrew Terrell Bershell came a month early; we said that he got too big for the house. We were wanting to name him Lewis Terrell Bershell Jr. But my father-in-law hated being call Junior and talked us out of it. So, we decided to do what my parents did: named him after his grandfather. Later, when Andrew was older, he wanted to know why he was not named after me. I could understand his point, because I wanted to know why I was not named Sammie Bershell III. I learned that my parents didn't know you could do that, by daddy being a junior they thought that that was it. My best friend growing up was named Ellis Whitmore III. I thought that was cool and always wondered why I wasn't the third.

After the birth of Andrew, Chris went back to work in the data processing operation; she got her old job back. With the increased income, we bought a new car and moved into a three-bedroom apartment. Mom, Dad, and Carolyn saved us childcare cost; they came over every night. I remember Chris telling me how they were with Jim's grandchildren. That was nothing compared to how they are with Nettie and Andrew.

We started the construction of our first home before the one-year lease was up on the three-bedroom apartment was completed. We chose a wooded lot to build on and only wanted enough trees removed to build the house and leave the rest in the woods. There were many small trees on the lot; the large trees that were cut down became firewood because the house would have a fireplace. Our little family really enjoyed watching the progress of our new home.

Our new home was completed, and there was a closing date scheduled. We had a moving crew of friends from work helping us move in, when we learned that the mortgage had been rejected. Now, we had a problem: we had completely moved out of our apartment into a house that we could not close on. The builder let us stay in the house until we fixed the problem—the problem was that the mortgage loan had been disqualified, because the car that Mattie owned was still counted on my credit as a loan. I had a Church bond that I was holding until it fully matured.

There was a member of the Church who was buying those bonds. This was an investment for him: he gave me what I needed to pay off the car, of which I did, and then, we met with Mattie at the Bureau of Motor Vehicles to sign the title over to her. This was also the very last time I would see her alive. We were able to close on the house. While living there, we took out the small trees necessary to make the backyard look like a park.

This was the reason we wanted the builder to let us remove the trees that we wanted; after adding a privacy fence around the backyard, the place was perfect. During the first Christmas in our new home, we had the whole family over. This house was perfect for the gathering. The kids had a great Christmas with all the presents they got. They were the only grandchildren and great-niece and nephew.

The only drawback with the trees was that a storm snapped a tall tree and dropped it on the roof of the house: this is where Dad was amazing. He came over and helped me put a tarp on the roof to cover the holes poked by the tree; other neighbors came over with chainsaws and cut up the tree. Now, that was a scary situation; the kids were at Mom and Dad's when the storm came thru, but Chris and I were in the house when it happened.

The subdivision we lived in was perfect for our kids: they were part of a group of little kids of the same age that played all over the neighborhood. All the parents in the neighborhood looked out for them while they played. Nowhere else that we have lived were our children so free to play and had so many friends.

Even though this was the perfect home and neighborhood, we decided to sell the house and move. The property was reaccessed, and our house payment went up to the point that we panicked. We decided to buy a cheaper house. This became a very bad idea, but our jobs got us off the hook by relocating us to Columbus, Ohio, when the Army pay was taken over by the Air Force system and relocated to Denver, Colorado.

We were displaced but were guaranteed jobs, unlike the private sector; government employees are treated differently, and not just left unemployed. The government took care of our move and the cost of relocating to Columbus, Ohio, which was our choice. Chris wanted to live somewhere else, other than here in Indiana.

At the time of our move, Chris was no longer a government employee; she had become a school bus driver for the Hamilton Southeastern schools—she and her sister Carolyn. They both went through the school bus driving program, were tested, and became license drivers of the Hamilton Southeastern Schools. I was so proud of how she could handle that big bus.

The government paid for my relocation from Indianapolis to Columbus, Ohio. Movers came in and boxed the whole house, then loaded the truck, and then moved it to a storage unit at Wright

Patterson Air Force Base. I was to go ahead and establish a place for my family. Chris wanted no part of that, so we all moved together. True to her word, she would never let me stay anywhere without my family. The government paid for our temporary lodging until we found our permanent lodging.

Chris received a temporary appointment to the Columbus finance and accounting center. This gave us the income needed to buy another house. Our house back in Indianapolis sold quickly. Our realtor showed us many houses, of which none were what we were looking for. We then decided to build another home.

When we moved to Columbus, Ohio, I became one of the ministers at the Love Zion Baptist Church. This was the first time since leaving the Junior Church at the Kingsley Terrance Church of Christ. I felt recognized as a minister. All other attempts had not achieved success as then. I had begun to feel that my divorce and remarriage had made me unworthy to be a youth minister. But this was not true; that was a phase of my life that was only connected to Mattie, and now, I was in a new phase with Chris and the kids, which was requiring that I move on and forget the past. Everything would be totally different.

The construction of our new home went according to plans, and before we knew it, we were living in our new home. This house was bigger than the other houses we lived in: it had a half basement and crawl space with gravel and plastic over the gravel. This new home was better than the others; it was perfect for our family.

As one of the ministers in the church, we would on the first Sunday of the month have dinner at one of our homes. The membership of this church was totally black, which cause a few problems for Chris, especially when it came to our son Andrew, who would not stay in the worship service. He would disappear and explore the huge old building. The older black ladies gave Chris the impression that she wasn't controlling him like she should, being white and all.

One of the problems with our children is this was the first church where I was required to sit on the pulpit with the other ministers. In the past, I was always a youth minister, and our children were not required to be in an adult worship service, which was a very boring two hours for children. We tried to create a Junior Church at Love Zion, but it didn't work because I was not allowed to become totally immersed in it as in other churches.

In the Churches of Christ, I did not need to be ordained or licensed, as a minister. In the United Methodist Church, I was a layman, and had not completed the process of ministry. I had been before the local board, had been referred to the district, had been before the district board, and had been assigned a supervisory pastor; all I lack was the educational requirements, which equal to a master's degree. This is where I would go no further, because my total commitment was to my family; I had almost not had children, and now that I did, nothing would be placed before them—not even what I believed to be my call to ministry.

When it came to ministry, I was in a unique situation. I didn't have the educational requirements for white churches, and in the black churches, I could not hoop (you see your best hoopers are also singers). But when it came to children, they have always been drawn to me all my life. When I was in school, one of the things we did was to run in possession. I never was chosen by my own age group, so I would create my own of the younger kids; I was in the fifth grade at this time. When I ran with my possess, the younger boys would just start running with us, when we got to where the battlefield was. I had a huge group of younger boys following me. It seems that the young boys just started running with us.

Chapter Five

O ur time in Ohio was where we really developed our lives together and learned the power of the coin. I used the term coin to explain what our connection to each other caused in our lives. What I am writing now is based upon what has happened in our lives. Our lives in Ohio was buried in my thirst for ministry: I became a fanatic about the subject. I had finally got the recognition base upon my terms, instead of the established set of standards by each church involved. Everything I did was filtered on the theology I was developing. I listened to certain preachers on the radio while at work; only listening to Christian music was a part of every activity of our church. As time went by, I had very little time for my family activities: I had added selling rainbow vacuums cleaner to my list of activities and then retired from my government job. As a vacuum cleaner salesman, my days started from 10 a.m. to 10 p.m. of which I drove up to one hundred miles a day, seeking sales opportunities.

On the other hand, Chris quit her government job again, to open a childcare center, in pursuit of her dreams. She had a child-care center of a combination of toddlers and our two children. This combination of ages was hard enough to manage, but when the key family that got her childcare started needed to have their son transported to a church preschool, this created an unsafe environment for the babies in her care. Her childcare had to be terminated. After the end of the daycare, she went back to driving school buses.

I was very successful as a rainbow vacuum cleaner dealer, to the point that I retired after twenty-six years of federal service. There was a lot of stress on my job; I was working twelve hours a day and dealing with a payment of a million dollars, which was locked up in the computer system. This situation had generated a congressional investigation. My division chief committed suicide: he parked his car in front of his church, soaked himself with gasoline, then set himself on fire.

The Columbus Finance and Accounting Center went through a reduction in force to accommodate the new building being built—employees with five years or less of service would be released, and the rest of us would be required to maintain the workload. To aid in the reduction, early retirements were offered of which I chose to take advantage of. With my seven years of military time, I retired after twenty-six years of federal service.

Now, I was able to devote full-time to my rainbow business and became one of our organization's top salespeople. I received an all-expense-paid trip to the rally in Dallas, Texas, where the new rainbow vacuum cleaner was unveiled in a spectacular presentation. This experience created a conflict for me, because as a rainbow dealer, I was being groomed to open a satellite office in the Columbus, Ohio, area. The guy who saw my potential and was preparing me for opening my office was divorced, and when he had time with his kids, you could tell how much he missed them being part of his life. This created a problem for me; I was not willing to sacrifice my time with my kids. I just could not see myself not being a part of my kids' lives every day.

There are times when opportunities present themselves that will cause us to achieve what we never thought would happen. These are the opportunities that cause some people to be wealthy, if the person is willing to do what is necessary; this was that time in my life. We do not rise to higher levels in life; others reach down and lift us up to where they are. This is what was happening to me in the rainbow business. The man that I was in Dallas with and who made sure I was involved in making the trip said to me, "If you place this business at the same level you do religion..." At this time in my life, and even now, I will not put anything before my family. I was still seeking to be a minister more than anything else. This is what Sammy had noticed about my commitment in life. The ability to be successful at whatever I chose to set as a priority was there. In Dallas, I spent time with people who made the kind of money that afforded them a level of life that I now had the tools to reach, and the man that I was there with was making it possible for me. Chris and I had tried many things to succeed. We once tried the envelope stuffing business; we received contact from the postmaster general about a chain letter that we thought was a form of lottery, which turned out that it was an address label company marking scheme. This was it, and this was the time that was presenting itself to us. The distraction of my full-time government employment was no longer there. There was only one more thing that held me back, and that was church.

After returning from Dallas, Texas, I was involved in a car crash while trying to get to a product demo. No one from the church came to the hospital as a show of support for my wife and family. We were so overjoyed to see Sammy show up at the hospital. I was just there to be checked out because of the impact of the crash. From this time on, we developed a different view of the church. Not long after Sammy was involved in a crash, and just as with me, only was shaken up. Then, a young lady in our rainbow sales organization was involved in a crash, of which she was killed. There are several ways these events can be interpreted. It was the will of God letting me know that I was being drawn away from his plan for my life. By using this interpretation, we must ask this question, "Why would God cause the death of a young mother to send a message to me?" The coined phrase "It's the will of God" is a terrible thing to say to someone that is hurting from a tragic event in their life. The loss of this young mother in our sales organization was hard on all of us and casted a dark shadow over our group.

After the unveiling of the new machine in Dallas, my ability to sell the machine diminished, because I had lost confidence in the integrity of the machine on a product demonstration to a man that was the owner of a large business that made HEPA filters. He told me that the new rainbow would have one, and it did. I had problems explaining it to my customers, causing me to feel that I was deceiving people. I sold a machine to a couple, where the husband didn't want his wife's income to be used to buy the machine, so that when they went to purchase a house their income debt ratio would not affect their ability to purchase the house. She wanted the machine so much that she privately went against his wishes and purchased the machine anyway. They kept the machine pass the three-day period to resend the purchase, and he wanted us to take the machine back. This alone with other situations cause me to decide to quit and become a school bus driver, for Groveport Madison schools, along with my wife Chris. Chris and I are again working together, which always happens, because we are never apart long.

At the end of the school year, we moved to Rockford, Illinois, where I was still chasing my desire to be ordained as a minister. It was the belief that my brother would get that done. We lived in Rockford for a year, in the worse house we had ever lived in. We lost the house in Ohio through bankruptcy, and my family felt that we always lived house-poor and on the white side of town. In Rockford, we lived on the west side where mostly black people lived. We rented a little house owned by a deacon of the church where my brother was the pastor.

We drove school buses for the Rockford public schools, of which we love doing, because we were back working together again. The time in Rockford was not good for us, in many ways. This was the second time I had lived close to my family, which was working out no better than when I went into the army. The goal of being ordained did not and was not going to happen. At the end of the school year, we decided to move back to Indiana, because it was determined that I had nothing in common with my family. During that year, I spent more time with Tommy, a fellow bus driver than my brother. Tommy became a big brother to me and my family. We got into serious archery, where Tommy taught me how to make my own arrows. We would travel to archery competitions on the weekends. My son Andrew and Tommy's grandson were also competing. The clash between my mother and I caused us to be moved out of her house. Living with her was also part of the arrangement that we made in moving to Rockford. Therefore, we ended up with that horrible rental house. Part of the situation was the house was located in an area that the city paid us to move because it was buying the property from the owner to accommodate the road that would go through the area and also paid our moving expenses. The deacon had another rental that was offered to us, but we had enough of these types of old houses. We decided to use the money to move back to Indiana.

Back in Indiana, things were different, while we were in Ohio, my sister-in-law Carolyn's cancer returned and was terminal this time. Dad's health had deteriorated to the point that he had become feeble. We are now entering the time when we started losing our parents and that generation. This is the period where we spent a lot of time in hospitals and attending funerals. There was a space of time after we lost Carolyn; then, Mom's brother-in-law Uncle Lawrence went into the hospital, and we lost him. Later, Mom's sister Aunt Deloris, a woman so large that the emergency medical team had to remove doors from her trailer and had to literally drag her down the hallway to get her out to the ambulance, was being taken to the hospital, before we lost her. Nettie was in junior high school and had to call 911 for Dad; he was taken to the hospital, and we lost him. There was a spot for each of us in the cemetery, including me. The arrangement was that Nettie would lay on the side of Carolyn, then Chris, then me, and then Andrew. This is the cemetery where Mom's family is.

My mother after battling leukemia, diabetes, and arthritis joined the members of our family whom we lost. After her death, I no longer had the drive to be an ordained minister or a minister of any kind. After I started preaching, she revealed to me that she prayed that if she had a first son he become a minister. Her son is a minister and is the pastor of the church she was a member of, and he is my brother, the son she raised. I was always considered to be the son of Mama and Papa, my great-grandparents, the same people that raised my father after his mother, my grandmother's death. My parents were only the vehicle to get me into the world, and never really were my parents. I grew up to be nothing like them in any way.

This is interesting, because Chris was raised by her parents, and she felt that she was not their child, and now that everyone was gone, she would never learn the truth. Somehow she felt that her Aunt Deloris was always hiding the truth from her: that she was really her mother. Aunt Deloris had no children but had a look of longing in her eyes when it came to Chris. Chris had noticed that Mom had always favored Carolyn over her. Carolyn had been an only child for four years before Chris was born; there were things that happened at Chris's birth that were questionable. Mom was in the hallway, and had not contact with her for four days, and Aunt Deloris was not allowed to see her for two years. Mom was not to have any more children after Carolyn, because of complications. These were the odd event that was present at the birth of Chris's birth. Then, there was the knowledge of Aunt Deloris's prior marriage. There's also the fact that Carolyn never had children or a relationship with anyone and Chris did. Is her feeling about this that of what the youngest child feels because they are always in the shadows of the oldest?

About the Author

Lewis was born in 1952 in Bastrop, Louisiana. His parents, Sammie, Jr., and Christella Bershell, were young, so Sammie, Jr.'s grandparents, Jimmie and Nettie Hall, raised the new baby. Lewis grew up in the south during the 1960s. Lewis graduated from Bastrop High School in 1970, the first integrated class. After high school, he enlisted in the Army. After seven years of active duty, he spent another nineteen years as a civilian employee, retiring in 1998. He followed his wife as a school bus driver. After twenty-two years, he retired again in 2020.